Anxiety and Panic Attack Solutions

A Guide to Dealing with Anxiety and Panic Attacks

S. K. Allen

Table of Contents

Introduction

Pretend for a moment that you are driving down a highway. All of a sudden, for no apparent reason, your heart begins to race. Your breathing becomes difficult. Feeling lightheaded, you grab the steering wheel and notice that your hands are sweating. A feeling of panic overcomes you. Your mind races as you try to grasp what is happening. You struggle to stay in control, but the harder you try, the more out of control you feel. You tell yourself, "Just stay calm!" But the panic continues to escalate. You try to distract yourself by listening to the car radio or focusing your attention on the traffic around you. Another wave of panic! Seconds pass like minutes. You think, *What if I pass out? Maybe this is a heart attack!*

Terrified, overwhelmed with a sense of impending doom, you head for the nearest exit in a desperate attempt to get help. Once off the freeway, the feeling gradually subsides, leaving you shaken and bewildered.

This episode could have taken place in a shopping mall, a church, your favorite restaurant, or any number of other places. You have experienced a panic attack. The symptoms may vary, but the reaction is the same—terror! Chances are, you associate the panic episode with the freeway and you begin to think: If it happens on the highway, it could happen elsewhere. As you become more and more concerned about recurring panic attacks, your symptoms occur more frequently and you avoid more and more places until your world becomes very small. Eventually, you may come to believe that the only safe place is within your own home. The nightmare has just begun. Helplessly caught up in a panic-avoidance cycle, you are now dealing with the phenomenon known as agoraphobia.

Chapter one

The Anxiety Disorders
What causes Anxiety Disorders?

Chapter one

The Anxiety Disorders

This book discusses five of the anxiety disorders recognized by the American Psychological Association: panic disorder with agoraphobia, panic disorder without agoraphobia, social phobia, simple phobia, and generalized anxiety disorder. Each of these is seen as a rather distinct problem, and each can be recognized by a set of more or less predictable characteristics.

Panic Disorder With Agoraphobia (PDA)

PDA, or simply agoraphobia, is the most common and most debilitating of the anxiety disorders. Many look at it as a "fear of fear," or more specifically, a fear of being trapped and unable to get help. Those of us with PDA experience recurring panic attacks that seem to come from out of the blue.

During a panic attack, some of the following symptoms can be present:

- Increased heart rate

- Dizziness or lightheadedness
- Faintness
- Increased respiration
- Sweating
- Tension in the stomach, neck, or shoulders
- Trembling hands or legs
- Weak knees
- Shortness of breath
- A feeling of suffocation
- Fatigue
- Difficulty swallowing
- *Blurred vision*
- Inability to concentrate
- Confusion
- A feeling of unreality
- A fear of dying
- A fear of going crazy
- A sense of impending doom

Although the first episode often takes place in a specific situation, the time and place of subsequent episodes may be unpredictable. As a result our lifestyle becomes very restricted. Feeling helpless and out of control, we are vulnerable to depression. PDA and depression often go together.

In order to feel safe or to protect ourselves from embarrassment, we avoid places where we think the unpredictable feelings of panic might occur. In extreme cases, this could mean quitting jobs and eventually becoming housebound. However, not all people who have agoraphobia become housebound. Many of us cleverly manage to conceal our fears day to day from family and friends to avoid ridicule and to protect ourselves from further shame. The plight of the agoraphobic is frightening, lonely, and bewildering.

Panic Disorder Without Agoraphobia

This problem is very similar to panic disorder with agoraphobia except that extensive avoidance does not take place. Also, fearful thoughts are usually limited to perceptions that our body is not functioning properly, that our health is unreliable, and that some sort of physical collapse may be imminent.

Social Phobia

Unlike agoraphobics, people with social phobia often experience the least anxiety when they are alone. They usually fear various situations which involve the presence of people. Bothersome situations include being in crowded public places, rooms, or vehicles; being in meetings, formal groups, or social gatherings; and giving a public presentation. Some common catastrophic thoughts include fears of becoming visibly anxious, being scrutinized closely and judged negatively, babbling or talking incoherently, and going through a severe breakdown during a public presentation. Social phobics may also experience panic attacks.

Simple Phobia

Those of us with simple phobias fear specific events or situations. Fears of specific animals or animal groups are among the most common. Also common is the fear of heights (acrophobia), which usually involves a fear of falling to one's death, or the fear of being hemmed in (claustrophobia), which can involve being in closed rooms, tunnels, airplanes, land vehicles, boats, elevators, and so on. Another set of phobias involves the fear of dying as a result of an automobile accident, drowning, or being struck by lightning.

Generalized Anxiety Disorder (GAD)

GAD involves persistent anxiety over a long period of time, with little respite. The intensity can sometimes stay high. Typically, those with GAD are stressed out about two or more major life problems (for example, work, personal finances, family, or illness). They feel that the problems are difficult to manage and that they have little control over them.

What Causes Anxiety Disorders?

Some researchers claim that people who experience recurring anxiety or panic attacks have a genetic predisposition to anxiety disorders. Other researchers see it as a behavioral problem. For some anxiety-panic sufferers, being told that their condition is hereditary gives them the feeling that they've just been given a life sentence. They see themselves as trapped in a situation over which they have no control, and they may give up trying to get well. Others feel a sense of relief, because seeing their problem as genetic frees them from shame.

Whatever the reason, the good news is that there is a way out of the anxiety or panic-avoidance cycle and, no matter how long we have suffered, it is possible for us to reach a point where the anxiety and panic are no longer trouble-some. One of the goals of this book is to help reassure yourself that you are still in control of your life, that there is something you can do about your anxiety and panic attacks, and that there is recovery.

The Role Of Environment

What kind of environment might predispose a person to an anxiety disorder? Perhaps they grew up with an overly critical parent or parent-figure whose high expectations gave them the feeling that they could do nothing right or that they were just not good enough. Or perhaps they had a parent who was overly protective, which gave them the message that they were living in an unsafe world and could not take care of themselves. They might also have feared abandonment or rejection.

Many anxiety and panic sufferers come from dysfunctional families. They may have been victims of alcoholism and learned fear at an early age. As children, they continually lived on the edge, not knowing what to expect from one day to the next. Their world was not safe, nor was it controllable. Subjected to abuse, they felt helpless and demoralized. They developed unhelpful coping strategies, such avoidance and repression of feelings, and felt a constant need to be on guard.

The Role Of Stress

Many people experienced significant levels of stress before experiencing major symptoms of anxiety. For some, stress built up over time until it reached a point where we could no longer cope. Those with anxiety problems have a style of coping with stressful events that persistently aggravates them. They tend to make unreasonable demands on themselves, telling themselves that they have to cope well and that because these particular events do not bother anyone else, they shouldn't bother them. But the more they try not to let things bother them, the more they aggravate themselves and the more stressful these events become.

Many people who develop anxiety problems have experienced a death in the family, severe illness, the loss of a friend, separation from a loved one, divorce,relocation, or any of a number of similar events.Loss seems to be a major theme.The fear of separation or isolation can stem from early childhood;we may have experienced difficulties resulting from the disruption of affectional bonds, especially those with parents. A history of separation anxiety and a problem with dependency on others are not uncommon. They usually cannot distinguish between the loneliness we feel as the result of a personal loss and the loneliness or isolation they might feel driving on the highway. Both can provoke anxiety or panic in people, but they fail to make the connection. They feel that the personal loss is understandable but tell themselves that panic on the freeway is inexcusable.

The Role Of Emotions

Those with panic disorders typically do not accept their negative feelings. In fact, they seem to be unaccepting of all feelings, whether negative or positive. It is important to encourage ourselves to be permissive of our feelings, regardless of what they might be, since being out of touch with them contributes much to our anxiety.

We have a very distinct way of interpreting our simplest thoughts and feelings - often seeing them as wrong, ridiculous, or irrational. We tell ourselves that we must be strong and that we must not give in to negative feelings, such as sadness, grief, or fear. The more unwilling we are to experience certain thoughts and feelings, the more we're troubled by them. We try hard to control them or get rid of them. But all this effort is exactly what gets us into trouble, since the need to control and get rid of them is the best recipe for continued aggravation and distress.

The Role Of Self-Talk

Those with anxiety disorders have a style of self-talk that demeans and dehumanizes themselves. It is non-permissive and shaming.For example, they might tell themselves,*"I shouldn't be feeling this way!"* Or *"This is ridiculous!"* The more they use this kind of self-talk, the more distressed they become and the more likely they are to experience anxiety or panic. Not realizing that their self-talk is counterproductive, that it acts against them, they try even harder to use the only strategies they are familiar with: avoidance, distraction, and being overly intellectual and analytical. The harder they try, the worse things get for them and the worse things get, the harder they try. They find themselves locked into a seemingly endless cycle of negative self-talk and distress.

The Role of Perfectionism

Perfectionism plays a large part in laying the groundwork for anxiety disorders. We spend much of our lives telling ourselves that we can't accept failure or perceived inadequacies. We develop and insist on high expectations and often feel that we never do enough or that what we do is not good enough. We do not accept ourselves, our thoughts, or our feelings; we adopt all-or-nothing ways of things. All of this places heavy demands on us. We use the same "perfectionistic" strategies in dealing with our anxiety problems. They are very complex, and our motives for using them sound extremely logical.

According to Judith Bemis in her book, "Embracing the Fear", the five major "perfectionistic" strategies are:

1. **Raising expectations**. These strategies compel us to generate very high expectations of doing well and are usually signalled by such expressions as *I must, I have to, I should, I've got to,* and *I can't*. Presumably, the higher our expectations, the better we will cope. For example: *I've got to go to the mall today! I just can't continue to avoid it anymore! And when I get there, I've got to do well! I can't allow myself to get anxious! I've got to control myself or else something awful might happen! I must never even think about escaping! That would be too shameful and unacceptable!* It is no wonder that even the simplest tasks become difficult.

2. **Absolutism**. These are all-or-nothing strategies. We presume that if we corner ourselves into a limited set of options, the "perfect" choice will be obvious. Therefore, our freedom of choice becomes highly restricted: *I've got to drive on the freeway today and do so without any trouble! I must have no anxiety whatsoever! I've got to go where I'm going without taking the easiest route!* With our choices so restricted it is no wonder that we often feel trapped by our thoughts and cannot make decisions or engage in problem solving.

3. **Acceleration**. Strategies of acceleration are based on the idea that the best way to do anything is to do it as quickly as possible. It doesn't matter if we fall flat on our face while doing it. We have little appreciation of the fact that often the fastest way of completing a task is to do it slowly and with clarity of mind.

4. **Control**. These are strategies of trying to keep Under control feelings and catastrophic thoughts that are perceived to be uncontrollable: *I can't let things get out of hand! If I do, then they will*

get even more out of hand, and that would be humiliating.

5. **Elimination**. Of the five, this strategy appears to be the most pervasive. It involves using avoidance, distraction, prevention, substitution, diversion, camouflage, denial, rationalization, minimization, and other strategies to "get rid of" unwanted feelings, thoughts, and behaviors. Of course, feelings, thoughts, and behaviors are not easily eliminated, and trying to do so merely makes us more troubled by them.

Other Factors

If suffering from a panic disorder, we often do not feel in charge of our lives. We feel helpless and do not assert ourselves in our relationships; we fail to establish boundaries and express our needs. Our self-esteem often depends on how we think other people judge us. To feel good about ourselves or to be accepted, we constantly seek the approval of others. Our low self-esteem and lack of self-confidence keep us from taking risks; we often feel stuck.

In many cases, life has become a treadmill that is moving faster than we can handle. Feeling pressured, we have a difficult time slowing down or taking time for ourselves. We continually tell ourselves that we have to hurry through various tasks, even the simplest ones. Is it any wonder that life has become unmanageable and that anxiety and panic have become a way of life?

Anxiety Disorders and Alcohol

People suffering from anxiety disorders in general, and agoraphobia in particular, appear to use chemicals, especially alcohol, to relieve their symptoms. It may be that agoraphobia, in many cases, follows attempts to relieve anxiety symptoms. One study found that as many as one-third of agoraphobics who are also alcoholics said they began drinking as a way of controlling their anxiety symptoms.

In a 1990 article, Kushner and colleagues suggested that there is a shared relation between alcohol and anxiety. A person may begin with the belief that drinking alcohol can alleviate anxiety, which leads to actually drinking, which leads to increased anxiety, which leads to further alcohol consumption. It may be that the more anxious people become, the more alcohol they feel they need to consume to alleviate their anxiety. And this reinforces their belief that alcohol reduces anxiety.

Another study reports that between 10 and 40 percent of alcoholics have a panic-related anxiety disorder, and that about 10 to 20 percent of people suffering from an anxiety disorder abuse either alcohol or other drugs. One interesting finding this study makes is that the majority of people who suffer from both alcoholism and an anxiety problem say that the anxiety problem came before the alcohol problem.

From this and similar studies, it is tempting to conclude that excessive use of alcohol and other substances has a harmful effect on anxiety-related problems.

Gaining a New Perspective

It is difficult for us to think that there's anything positive about an anxiety disorder. It feels so debilitating that we can perceive it only as an indication of abnormality and dysfunction. For example, agoraphobia is associated with a great deal of emotional, social, and occupational impairment. The quality of life of an agoraphobic person is not enviable.

From a different perspective, however, there is much about agoraphobia that is positive. First, anxiety is essentially a normal response to stress. Once this is accepted, even intense or persistent anxiety and yes, even panic attacks - can be seen as serving a useful function in our lives (although we are unlikely to see this function when we are persistently being overwhelmed by anxiety). Can you imagine yourself in a life-threatening situation and not experiencing an intense anxiety reaction?

The usual response to this argument is that the fears of those who suffer from anxiety disorders are not experienced in life-threatening situations, that their fears are irrational and serve no useful function. Such is the perspective of someone suffering from agoraphobia. But let's look at it from another perspective.

Agoraphobic fears have almost nothing to do with situations that are life-threatening; the situations do not pose a threat to our health or personal safety. A simple look at the kinds of situations that are typically feared by agoraphobics reveals that the threat posed is an emotional one; specifically, we feel threatened with a loss of self-esteem. When entering a feared situation, such as a shopping mall, most of our thoughts are focused on whether or not we will cope well - whether we will have uncomfortable feelings or "abnormal" thoughts, or engage in shameful behaviors that will compromise our self-esteem. The catastrophic thoughts of a typical agoraphobic (*What if I panic? What if I faint? What if I lose control and scream?*) essentially involve fears of loss of self-esteem. What we are really saying is I had better not behave this way, for such behavior is disgraceful and humiliating. Even thoughts of having a heart attack or a stroke, or of dying, can be related to our sense of self-worth, since being alive and healthy are inextricably linked with how we value ourselves.

The gist is that the shame-based quality of our fears can alert us to their usefulness, to the emotional meanings represented by our fears. For example, if we have a panic attack while shopping at a mall or driving on a freeway, our response may be one of extreme misery; we see such reactions as meaningless or as signs of personal defectiveness. However, the panic attack can serve as an important signal to alert us that difficult issues in our lives are in pressing need of attention, and that perhaps the time has come to start taking risks to bring about important changes.

Chapter two

The Beginning of the Recovery Process.

We hate our problem with a passion; we hate our fears, our avoidance behaviors, our catastrophic thoughts, and our dependency on other people to help us do the simplest things. The problem is so complex and causes so much grief that we are unlikely to see any merit in our fears and anxiety. However as our journey to recovery begins and we start to make sense of what is happening to us, the problem becomes less and less threatening and at some point can even be seen as a friend. In recovery, we often reach a point at which we are better off than we've ever been in our entire lives.

What is Recovery?

It is difficult for those of us who suffer from panic or chronic anxiety to believe that life could ever again be normal, especially if we have struggled with anxiety problems for a long time. But it is possible. The problem is that we often try to get better by using the same strategies that helped cause the problem: shaming ourselves, being intolerant of our thoughts and feelings, and trying hard to be perfect.

Typically, those of us who suffer from anxiety problems have extremely unrealistic expectations of ourselves. So it is natural for us to view our recovery with similar unrealistic expectations of ourselves: we want a perfect recovery as soon as possible. The more perfect we insist our recovery should be, however, and the more we try to hurry it, the more disappointed we are likely to become in our efforts to get well.

Since anxiety problems become entrenched in our daily lives, and since our self-talk is an indelible part of how we think and how we cope with various aspects of our lives, it is likely that very little will change at first. Recovery takes time, and the more time we give ourselves, the more stable and long-lasting our recovery will be.

When we develop a permissive attitude about our panic attacks, when we're able to let go of our fear of them, they lose their power and occur less and less often, until we no longer find ourselves waiting for that next wave of panic from out of the blue. As we gain more confidence and take more risks, we focus less and less on our anxiety and panic attacks. We no longer need to label ourselves "agoraphobic." We can now see ourselves as normal people; the anxiety or agoraphobia becomes an inconsequential part of our total self-image.

Recovery does not mean we'll never feel anxious again; no one can expect to be completely anxiety-free. But the anxiety will diminish and become much more manageable. The more we lower our expectations for a perfect recovery, the stronger a recovery we can actually bring about. The more time we give ourselves, the sooner we will recover. Such inconsistencies are difficult to accept and understand. At first, they seem neither logical nor helpful. However, as you read this book, the many inconsistencies of the recovery process will become more understandable. And this understanding will make the recovery process easier.

Recovery means more than being free of panic or anxiety; it also means personal growth and awareness. In recovery, we look back and realize that we have made it through a very difficult time. This realization leaves us with a feeling of great accomplishment. We gain valuable insights and learn coping skills that can change our lives.

If the ideas and strategies within this book could be condensed into one word, it would be *allow*. Throughout this book, you will be encouraged to allow your thoughts, feelings, anxiety - and even panic. You are encouraged to accept them at times and even invite them. Nowhere will you be told that you must do something about your anxiety. Instead of using words like *should, must*, and *have to*, which are words that belong to a coping style that promotes unmanageable anxiety, we encourage a more adaptive style of coping that is more permissive of failure and puts less emphasis on obligation and the need to perform perfectly.

Managing Anxiety

The ideas laid out in this book differ from other anxiety management programs in that it encourages a comprehensive permissive approach in dealing with anxiety. It allows us to experience the process of recovery without putting demands on us. In other words, it gives us permission to have the problem. It does not give us the message that we *have to* relax or that we *must* stop thinking catastrophic thoughts. It does not tell us that we must *force* ourselves to generate positive affirmations that are both unbelievable and impossible to internalize. Nor does it insist we *compel* ourselves to never withdraw from an unmanageable situation. These demands fit in to kind of self-talk that has already contributed to our problems with anxiety. To many, the ideas in this book may seem paradoxical and irrational, but they involve a most natural and effective approach to recovery.

Relaxation

One of the most important ideas in this program is that we needn't be insistent on relaxation. This is not to say that relaxation isn't helpful. Naturally, a comfortable state of relaxation is desirable, especially since a panic attack seems inconsistent with relaxation. However, for those with an anxiety disorder, telling themselves that we *have to* get hold of ourselves or that we *have to* relax only adds more pressure to their anxiety state. When we find relaxation difficult, we feel we have failed at a task anyone should be able to accomplish. What we need to do, in fact, is to *learn how to be anxious*. The first step in learning how to relax is letting go of the need to relax and allowing the anxiety to be there. In other words, we first need to give ourselves permission to have the problem. Then we can begin to do something about it.

The Escape/Avoidance Problem

It is true that we often escape from situations in which we are anxious or in which we experience a panic attack. It is also true that by following this experience, we often avoid that same situation. Eventually, similar situations - often less threatening than the original - now cause fear. As we continue to avoid, our world becomes smaller, resulting occasionally in unwillingness to venture outside the safety of home. A typical situation is that of the agoraphobic who experiences a panic attack at a large mall and escapes the mall, vowing never to return again. Soon he or she avoids all large malls, then avoids smaller shopping centers, since anxiety or panic attacks could occur there also. Finally, over a period of time, even the neighborhood grocery store is avoided.

It might appear that all we would need to do is refrain from escaping and avoiding feared situations. Unfortunately the answer is not that easy. We usually try very hard not to escape from feared situations, and if we do, we try equally hard not to avoid them later on. The instructions we give ourselves are complex: on one hand, we tell ourselves we cannot stay and therefore we have to leave; but on the other hand, we tell ourselves that we cannot leave - that would be shameful and cowardly - and so we have to stay.

It is impossible to stay in a place and leave it at the same time. And yet this is exactly what we are forcing ourselves to do. Since all the possible options are ruled out, we are left with no choices. This is a classic double-bind situation. The result is that we feel trapped, unable to stay and unable to leave. And when we feel trapped we are likely to experience panic. This is the most plausible reason panic attacks are so likely to occur in feared situations. This is also why escape and avoidance behaviors are so persistent and cannot be stopped by simply telling ourselves to do so.

The solution lies in seeing that both remaining in and leaving the feared situation are equally acceptable. It is not enough to encourage ourselves to stay in a feared situation, for that deals with only half the problem. It is equally important for us to realize that we truly are able and free to leave a feared situation any time we wish. Once we grant ourselves permission to leave, staying gradually becomes easier, for a major obstacle will have been removed.

Catastrophic Thoughts

There is a certain kind of fear, often called a fear of fear, which has a catastrophic quality about it. It is usually signalled by the phrase "What it?" For example: *What if I go to the shopping mall and I faint?* Or, *What if I drive on the freeway, have a panic attack, lose control and cause an accident!* Such thoughts are alarming, and there are many who believe we should learn to control such thoughts.

Such thoughts are harmless in themselves, even if they cause alarm or discomfort. In fact, that is exactly what they should do. It is not a bad idea to have a catastrophic thought about getting into an accident on the freeway; such thoughts could alert us to the need to be extra careful while driving. But what is troublesome about catastrophic thoughts is that they occur with such frequency. They also seem to have a life of their own. The more we try to control them or eliminate them, such as by distracting ourselves from them, the more troublesome they seem to become. Perhaps they are so frequent and so automatic because we try so hard not to have them and not to be alarmed by them.

When we have catastrophic thoughts, much more than mere thought is taking place. Our minds become very busy at this point and start to apply deep interpretations to these thoughts and devise strategies for dealing with them. One example of a deep interpretation is the idea that such thoughts are abnormal or defective: *Why am I having such thoughts? They are ridiculous! I shouldn't think this way!* There is no compelling reason why any of us should think this way but the fact is that we do think this way about our catastrophic thoughts. If we were to examine the self-talk in this paragraph, we would notice that it has a common theme: *shame.*

In brief, here are thirteen anxiety management strategies suggested by Bemis that we will be elaborating on:

1. We will try to accept the fact that we sometimes feel out of control of our lives because of feelings of anxiety or panic. By accepting the fact that we have an anxiety disorder, without passing judgment on ourselves, we have taken a major step in recovery.

2. Our self-talk, which tends to be shaming and non-permissive, has been partly responsible for our anxiety or panic. It continues to be a problem because it affects the intensity and duration of these feelings. It will help if we practice an inner dialogue that is nurturing. We might begin by giving ourselves permission to be anxious.

3. We will try to allow the sensations of anxiety or panic, not resisting them but just letting them happen. It will help if we do not attach danger to these feelings.

4. When feeling anxious, we will try to slow down, not only in our actions but in our thinking as well. When we feel a need to rush ahead, it will help if we try to focus on the moment.

5.

   With the onset of intense anxiety or panic, our first reaction is to try to stay in control. It will help if we practice letting go; the less we attempt to stay in control, the more in control we will feel.

6. We will try to take risks rather than continually avoid places and situations where we feel anxious. It will help if we reassure ourselves that we are not in any danger and that we can function well even when we're uncomfortable.

7. When "catastrophizing" with the what-ifs, we will try to be permissive of them and not fight them. It will help to realize that they are only thoughts and that chances are they will not happen. It might also help to affirm that we carry our safety within.

8. We will try to develop a more helpful attitude toward our anxiety disorder by learning more about it, thus removing the veil of mystery. By talking about it, we also lift the burden of a deep, dark secret.

9. When approaching a situation where we feel anxious, we will try to take it one step at a time, keeping our expectations low. It will help if we think of it as an opportunity to practice.

10. We will try to accept setbacks as a normal and necessary part of our recovery, trying to see them as temporary. It might help to remind ourselves that even though we feel as if we're starting over, we never really go back to square one.

11. We will try to take the time limit out of our recovery, seeing it as open-ended. It will help if we try to accept where we are right now without comparing ourselves with past progress, and at the same time, try to be accepting of the possibility of any future anxiety.

12. During our process of recovery, we can reach a point where we no longer anticipate the occurrence of panic attacks. When we no longer care if we panic, the attacks will eventually subside.

13. As we gain a better understanding of our anxiety problem and move ahead in our recovery, we can continue to benefit by reaching out to others who need support and encouragement.

Listening to Our Inner Dialogue

Inner dialogue is a vital part of this recovery program, since our self-talk has played an important part in precipitating and maintaining our anxiety problem. What we say to ourselves at the onset of a panic attack can affect its severity and duration. It can also affect our perception of the problem itself. For instance, if we see our anxiety or panic as shameful or unacceptable, we will tap into a self-shaming and non-permissive inner dialogue, also known as "Crap-talk." For example, *This is terrible! I shouldn't have this problem! There must be something terribly wrong with me!* All of these thoughts are alarming and only serve to add anxiety to an already anxious state.

The essence of Crap-talk is an abusive and dehumanizing system of managing our life. It is intolerant of imperfection and failure and insistent on perfection and approval. It is this system that constantly creates problems for us.

Recovery depends on being able to set up a different way of managing our feelings, thoughts, and behaviors. This new system, labeled "Good-talk," needs to compete with the old system (Crap-talk). Good-talk cannot replace the old system because it is impossible to get rid of. In fact, the more we try to do that, the more troublesome the Crap-talk becomes. The biggest problem with the Crap-talk is that it has become highly ingrained in our personality. Therefore, it is likely to persist and to be automatic for some time to come. The best we can do at first is to try to generate the new system as a competing way of interpreting and dealing with problems in general, and with our anxiety disorder in particular.

The new system offers ideas to counter those of the old system. It processes information about ourselves and the world around us in a fundamentally different way; it is a self-nurturing and non-shaming way of interpreting events. It is highly tolerant of the self and permissive of imperfection and failure. Good-talk does not insist on perfection, or try to get rid of or control anything. Rather, it tries to be allowing of scary feelings, catastrophic thoughts, avoidance behavior, and even relapses. It is a highly humanizing voice that accepts us as we are, including our perceived imperfections and our catastrophic thoughts.

One of our first tasks is to become as familiar as possible with our Crap-talk. As we do, the connection between our Crap-talk and our distress becomes increasingly clear. At some point the question arises as to what to do about the Crap-talk: Do we control it? Do we get rid of it? If we were to follow such an approach, we would be dealing with our Crap-talk through more Crap-talk. A more effective approach is to incorporate a more nurturing inner dialogue (Good-talk) to directly compete with the Crap-talk, so that there is some balance between the two.

At first this new system will seem to be almost impossible to get going, and the old system will keep on operating and keep making us miserable. But this is to be expected. Slowly and gradually, however, the Good-talk will become internalized; it will become the natural way of coping with events. When this happens, we will have reached an important point in the recovery process.

Lifestyle Awareness

Each anxiety management strategy and its related inner dialogue corresponds to a lifestyle awareness topic, which allows us to see a correlation between how we deal with our anxiety or panic and how we deal with everyday life events.

The lifestyle awareness discussion does not give advice, nor does it tell us how to make changes in our lives. Its purpose is to raise our level of awareness of how we deal with everyday life situations and how this affects our anxiety level. In most cases it simply re-frames the situation so we can see it from a more helpful perspective. In some cases it suggests an alternative approach.

Whereas the anxiety management strategies help us manage our symptoms, the lifestyle awareness topics make us aware of possible environmental sources of anxiety and panic. The goal is to gain a better understanding of how we feel about ourselves and how we relate to others. We often discover that we are stuck in some area of our life, whether it's our lifestyle, career, relationship, or belief system. As we grow in this awareness, we begin to see that there is a relationship between our feeling of helplessness and our anxiety. We come to realize that we have options that can help us make the desired changes in our lives. During our recovery we become more and more aware that panic attacks do not form out of the blue - they are there for a reason.

Here are the thirteen topics of Lifestyle Awareness:

1. We are aware that we can be our own worst critic. It will help if we can try to be less self-critical by being more gentle with ourselves, accepting our limitations as well as our strengths.

2. We are aware that it will help to practice a nurturing inner dialogue, one that is more permissive and accepting of ourselves. We

might begin by being aware of the "shoulds" in our self-talk.

3.   We are aware of the importance of being in touch with and expressing our feelings. It will help if we try to allow ourselves to experience and express them without judgement or denial.

4.   We are aware that we have a tendency to take life at a fast pace. It will help if we try to slow down, make fewer demands on ourselves, and take time to experience the present.

5.   We are always aware that we sometimes feel out of control of our lives, which can leave us feeling trapped and helpless. We will try to let go, allow for more spontaneity, and see ourselves as having options.

6.   We are aware that we often choose avoidance as a way of dealing with difficult situations. It would be more helpful to try to work through these difficulties. If we cannot bring about a change, it will help if we try to

generate a new perception of the situation so that we will not feel trapped or helpless.

7. We are aware that our tendency to "cata-strophize" makes it difficult to be receptive to positive outcomes. It will help if we are permissive of our thoughts, both positive and negative, rather than feeling that we have to block them out or replace them with other thoughts.

8. We are aware that we sometimes avoid pro-cessing difficult events in our lives by not thinking about them or by distorting their meaning. It will help if we take a good look at them and try to see the meaning they have for us.

9. We are aware of our need for perfection. It will help if we allow ourselves to be average rather than to continually strive for perfec-tion. We might remind ourselves that mak-ing mistakes does not have to affect our self-worth.

10. We are aware that we have a difficult time dealing with failure, seeing it as further evidence of low self-worth. It will help if we give ourselves the freedom to fail, considering it an opportunity for growth.

11. We are aware that it helps to live one day at a time, while slowly coming to terms with the past and letting the future take care of itself.

12. We are aware that we have difficulty being flexible and that we tend to see things in all-or-nothing terms. It will help if we try to be less absolute in our thinking, allowing more flexibility in our lives.

13. We are aware that we feel better when we are actively involved, whether we are working, helping others, or pursuing leisure-time activities.

Chapter Three

Strategy No. 1 - *Accepting our Anxiety Disorder*

We will try to accept the fact that we sometimes feel out of control of our lives because of feelings of anxiety or panic. By accepting the fact that we have an anxiety disorder, without passing judgment on ourselves, we have taken a major step in recovery.

Acceptance begins with admitting that we have an anxiety disorder, one that in some cases has precipitated a vicious circle of panic and avoidance. Acceptance means facing the fact that there is no immediate cure, and no miracle drug at hand. It means realizing that our symptoms will most likely persist for some time; they will not go away just because we want them to. Denying that we have a problem, trying not to think about it, or telling ourselves how unacceptable it is, tends only to frighten and confuse us more and increase the feeling of being trapped.

As we move through this maze of fear and confusion, we are consumed with a sense of impending doom, convinced that there is something terribly wrong with us. Because of the nature of our symptoms, we can spend a great deal of time and energy on doctors and medical tests, trying to find a physical cause for our problem, only to be told that we are in good health and that perhaps our problem is emotional. When it is suggested that we seek professional psychological help, we become even more alarmed. We feel that having an emotional problem or seeing a therapist is shaming and stigmatizing. Somewhere along the way we have been given the message that we should be in control of our emotions.

For several reasons, we hang on to the belief that we are dealing with a physical problem. The intensity of symptoms convinces us that this has to be more serious than a case of nerves. We also believe that a physical illness is so much easier to fix: psychotherapy could take years just to get to the cause of the problem. Finally, seeing the symptoms as physical rather than emotional tends to alleviate our feeling of shame. Unfortunately, focusing exclusively on the physical can slow down the recovery process. Trying to get a new perspective on the situation and adopting a more permissive inner dialogue can be very helpful. Giving ourselves permission to have this problem is the first step in accepting our anxiety. It might help if we remind ourselves that no one is entirely free of problems. Some people have tension headaches or a chronic illness; we get a rush of adrenaline at unexpected times. So be it! The more we can see our problem as normal for our situation and the more we can accept it, the better. Those who are diagnosed early are fortunate. However, just because some of us have suffered with an anxiety disorder longer does not necessarily mean that it will take years of therapy to recover.

Once we know what we are dealing with, it is advisable to find a therapist who specializes in treating anxiety disorders. A support group that is well-facilitated and based on a structured program is also helpful. When we are in contact with others who face the same problem, we no longer feel so isolated and alone.

Learning about our anxiety disorder is essential, as it is difficult to be accepting when we do not know what is happening to us. It might take some time before we truly accept that we have this problem. Merely telling ourselves that we do accept it will not necessarily make our symptoms go away, at least not at first. Sometimes we will be able to accept, and other times we won't. In the beginning, the best we can do is to try to live with the discomfort. However long it might take, accepting the fact that we have an anxiety disorder and are still feeling okay about ourselves constitutes a major step in our recovery.

Listening To Our Inner Dialogue:

Non-acceptance/Acceptance

We tell ourselves that having this problem is unacceptable. It is shameful and therefore not permissible. Defects of character are not to be tolerated. If we allow such defects to be there, they will only get worse. Since non-permissive self-talk is highly internalized, acceptance will not come easily. We can, however, try to be more accepting of what is happening to us; we can adopt a more nurturing inner dialogue to balance the Crap-talk and the Good-talk.

Crap-Talk: Non-acceptance	Good-talk: Acceptance
1. This is ridiculous, stupid and crazy! I shouldn't have this problem.	1. Even though this might seem stupid or crazy, it's not. This is all a part of having an anxiety disorder.
2. What's wrong with me? This isn't normal!	2. I have a panic disorder. The feelings I'm having are normal for what I'm dealing with. It will help if I can be accepting of that.
3. Why am I feeling this way? I'm an adult and I shouldn't have these fears.	3. These feelings are part of having an anxiety problem, and it's okay to have them. Shaming myself will only make matters worse.
4. My friends and family will think I'm crazy.	4. This problem is difficult for other people to understand. I'll try to feel okay about my self regardless of what others might think.
5. I don't see anyone else dealing with something like	5. Everyone deals with something. For me it is a

this. Why me?	chronic fear of intense anxiety or panic attacks. So be it!
6. I'm so embarrassed about this. What if someone finds out?	6. It's okay to be phobic. I don't have to be embarrassed about it. The more I can give myself permission to be this way, the less of a problem it will be.

Lifestyle Awareness: *Accepting Our Limitations*

We are aware that we can be our own worst critic. It will help if we can try to be less self-critical by being more gentle with ourselves, accepting our limitations as well as our strengths.

Raising Our Level of Awareness

1. We tend to allow other people to make mistakes, but we are quick to judge our actions.	1. We might try to be more gentle with ourselves, by being less self-critical and giving ourselves more freedom to make mistakes. We might remind ourselves that our mistakes will not affect our self-worth.
2. We often focus on our limitations, feeling that what we do just isn't good enough.	2. We will try to recognize our strengths, even though we know this will be difficult. It will also help if we can be more accepting of our limitations.
3. We sometimes feel inferior and compare ourselves unfavorably with others.	3. Rather than putting ourselves down, we could try to accept and appreciate ourselves and our good qualities.

4. We worry about how we're viewed by others. (Criticism confirms any negative feelings we might have about ourselves.)

4. It will help if we remind ourselves that our concern isn't so much about what other people might think about us, but how we feel about what people might think about us, and how we feel about ourselves.

Chapter Four

Strategy No. 2: *Practicing A Self-Nurturing Inner Dialogue*

Our self-talk, which tends to be shaming and non-permissive, has been partly responsible for our anxiety or panic. It continues to be a problem because it affects the intensity and duration of these feelings. It will help if we practice an inner dialogue that is nurturing. We might begin by giving ourselves permission to be anxious.

Underneath our anxiety is an inner dialogue that is intolerant and critical of ourselves. Seeing our anxiety or panic as unacceptable, we belittle ourselves. We accuse ourselves of being irrational and tell ourselves that we have to do something about our problem. Our inner dialogue says, *Figure out what makes you anxious and get rid of it or change it.* The same holds true for our catastrophic thoughts, our avoidance behavior, and our setbacks. This non-permissive and shaming Crap-talk is a self-degrading approach to dealing with this and other problems. It would help to be more aware of our Crap-talk and to try to incorporate a more nurturing inner dialogue, Good-talk.

Good-talk is a highly permissive coping style. It allows us to have intense anxiety and panic attacks, to have catastrophic thoughts, and to go through setbacks. It allows us to have feelings of discouragement, disappointment, and depression. Good-talk does not come naturally to us, since our inner dialogue is permeated with Crap-talk. Crap-talk is largely responsible for our difficulties with anxiety and panic. Once we realize this, we might think that the answer is quite simple - all we have to do is replace the Crap-talk with the Good-talk. I repeat.....

Crap-talk is largely responsible for our difficulties with anxiety and panic. Once we realize this, we might think that the answer is quite simple - all we have to do is replace the Crap-talk with the Good-talk. However, since Crap-talk is so internalized it is not easy to rid ourselves of it. What we can do at first is listen to our Crap-talk and appreciate the extent to which it creates problems for us. Then we can try to generate some Good-talk, with the hope of establishing a dialogue between our Crap-talk and our Good-talk, between our non-permissive and our permissive thoughts.

What we say to ourselves when we are feeling anxious or at the onset of panic can make a difference to how we handle the feared situation. No matter how many times we have had these feelings, our first reaction has been to ask ourselves, *What's happening to me?* We then come up with any number of frightening answers. The question itself signals danger, and our inner dialogue continues to frighten us as we react to the mounting panic. Our response is to become alarmed by the fearful thoughts. This brings in more alarm, which sets off a complex cycle of Crap-talk and escalating catastrophic thoughts until we feel out of control.

We use this kind of self-talk because we don't understand what is happening to us. After all, we have good reason to be alarmed when feelings of such intensity seem to come out of nowhere. What would help is to try to make sense of what is happening in a simple and accurate way. e.g. *I'm anxious because of the stressful events that are going on in my life*, or, *I'm anxious because I have an anxiety problem.*

Making sense of our anxiety is not the same as being extremely rational, analytical, or intellectual. It is a simple, non-shaming way of dealing with this problem. We want to understand why we're anxious. We then want to look at it and tell ourselves that it's all right to have these feelings. If we can approach the task of understanding our problem in ways that are simple and more or less accurate, we will be on our way toward demystifying the problem. As we improve our understanding and awareness of how anxiety and phobias work, we are also better able to come up with a more nurturing way of talking to ourselves. Adopting an inner dialogue that is supportive and non-shaming helps us in our recovery.

Listening To Our Inner Dialogue:
Non-permissive/Permissive

Being unaccepting and intolerant of our unwanted thoughts, feelings, and behaviors seems like a logical and helpful strategy: the less tolerant we are, the more motivated we will be to eliminate them. Unfortunately, it is not that easy. Such a strategy is not only ineffective but also often leads to reinforcement of the unwanted thoughts, feelings, and behaviors. On the one hand, doing battle with them aggravates them and intensifies our fears; on the other hand, simply allowing them to run their course dilutes their importance. We can start by being more permissive of our anxiety and by encouraging ourselves to become more tolerant of whatever we experience - especially of ourselves and our perceived deficiencies.

Crap-talk:Non-permissive	Good-talk: Permissive
1. What's wrong with me? Why am I so anxious?	1. I'm probably anxious because _ _ (Offer a simple explanation, e.g., I didn't sleep well last night, my job is very stressful these days, I need to slow down.)

2. This shouldn't be happening to me! I must be dying (or passing out, going crazy, etc.)!

2. I'm having a panic attack. It's only the thought of dying that is frightening me. It's all right to have frightening thoughts. I'm not in any physical danger.

3. I can't go on like this! I just have to get hold of myself!

3. Chances are this feeling isn't going to go away just because I want it to. I'll try to be open to the thought that I just might be uncomfortable for a while.

4. This is ridiculous! It's all in my head. I've got to pull myself together!

4. I'm really being hard on myself. I don't have to do anything other than just let the fearful thoughts (anxiety) happen. Sometimes the best I can do is to muddle through and then try to be okay with that.

5. This is terrible! Nothing seems to be working I just can't stand this anymore!

5. This is very difficult, but I may be trying too hard. It will help if I allow these feeling to just be there and perhaps remind myself that "this too shall pass."

Lifestyle Awareness: *Being Less Self-Critical*

We are aware that it will help to practice a nurturing inner dialogue, one that is more permissive and accepting of ourselves. We might begin by being aware of the "shoulds" in our self-talk.

Raising Our Level of Awareness

1. Our self-talk has played a major role in our anxiety problem. We continue to use non-permissive strategies. For example, we tell ourselves we shouldn't have certain feelings, that it's not okay to express our needs or make certain decisions in our lives.

1. It will help if we try to adopt a more nurturing inner dialogue, one that is permissive and accepting of ourselves rather than critical and judgmental.

2. Our self-talk is permeated with "shoulds" that do not allow any options.

2. We might try to think in terms of "It would be nice if—" or "I would like to—"

3. We sometimes verbally abuse ourselves with such adjectives as silly, ridiculous, and irrational.

3. We might start trying to recognize and appreciate our fine qualities, being more receptive to an accepting and supportive inner dialogue. But even more important, we can try to accept any perceived deficiencies or inadequacies. The more accepting we are of these, the better we will feel about ourselves.

The more we can give ourselves permission to be uncomfortable, the better. So often we test ourselves by seeing how well we can do in feared situations. Our self-talk tends to say, *Let's see if I can do this without feeling anxious*. It would be more helpful to say, *I will most likely be anxious, since this is where I usually have difficulty. I'll try to see this as an opportunity to practice allowing any anxiety I might experience.*

Chapter five

Strategy N o. 3: *Allowing the Sensations of Anxiety or Panic*

We will try to allow the sensations of anxiety or panic, not resisting them but just letting them happen. It will help if we do not attach danger to these feelings.

There is nothing easy about "allowing" or "going with" the feeling when dealing with unmanageable anxiety or riding the wave of a panic attack. As our anxiety builds in intensity, we find ourselves fighting it every step of the way. We feel that the more we tense up and hang on, the more successful we will be in warding off the uncontrollable feelings. Unfortunately, the more we resist them, the more anxious we become, and we find ourselves helplessly caught up in a vicious circle of fear and panic. All thoughts of allowing or going with the feeling are quickly abandoned. With each strange sensation, we're quick to analyze what we think might be happening to us, and the more we focus on these thoughts, the more frightened we become. We feel that we are truly in some kind of danger - a perfectly valid feeling. However, an awareness of what is really happening will be helpful at this point. What we are dealing with is the thought of what we're afraid might happen, not the actual event. And it is the thought that is causing us to panic or to experience intense anxiety. By telling ourselves this - reassuring ourselves that it is only a feeling and that we are not in any physical danger - we can recognize the panic for what it is and then give ourselves permission to experience it.

The key to this strategy is the phrase "There is no danger!" Once we are at least somewhat sure of this fact (we're never really completely convinced), we're in a better position to work with the feelings themselves. After all, if we really think that we're going to make a fool of ourselves, we will be somewhat reluctant to just let it happen. Or if a feeling of impending doom convinces us that we're in some kind of danger, we're going to have a difficult time focusing on words such as *accept* and *allow*. Feelings of panic or intense anxiety are difficult enough to deal with when we recognize them for what they are. So until we can reassure ourselves that we are not in any danger, we're in for a rough ride.

When we stop focusing on the physical symptoms and realize it is only a thought that triggers the anxiety or panic, we find it's a little easier to accept, allow, and go with the feeling. Sometimes this means doing nothing at all, because no matter what we try, it just doesn't seem to help. It is important to be okay with that - in other words, to give ourselves permission to muddle through the best we can and to allow the frustration that goes with muddling. Fretting over the fact that nothing seems to be working, and then fretting over the fact that we are frustrated because nothing seems to be working, only adds to our stress.

We could try to see the next onset of anxiety or panic as a reaction to a thought and reassure ourselves that we are not in any physical danger. It will help if we give ourselves permission to have the symptoms without over-analyzing them or trying to distract ourselves. We can also rely on helpful coping strategies, whether that means allowing and going with the feeling or just muddling through!

Listening to Our Inner Dialogue:

Non-permissive/Permissive

We tell ourselves that certain feelings are shameful or unacceptable and must be done away with. Otherwise, they'll just go on forever. The idea is that the more strenuously we try, the more efficiently we'll get rid of things. As logical as that might sound, it doesn't work that way in this particular situation. The paradox is, the less effort we put forth, the more efficient we'll become in achieving our goal.

Crap-talk:	Good-talk: Permissive
Non-permissive	
1. I have to stop being so anxious! I must relax!	1. I'll try to allow the anxiety to be there. I do not have to force myself to relax.
2. If I don't do something about this anxiety, it's really going to get out of hand.	2. It is better if I let go and allow the anxiety to do what it wants, without my trying to stop it.
3. I feel like I'm going to pieces. I've got to get a hold of myself!	3. I'm not really going to pieces. I only feel that way. It will help if I can allow that feeling.
4. There must be something terribly wrong with me. This just isn't normal.	4. There's nothing wrong with me other than the fact that I'm feeling anxious.
5. I'm letting this get the best of me. Maybe if I just don't think about it, it will go away.	5. Trying hard not to think about it doesn't always work. It's better if I can just stay with the feeling and try not to fight it.

Lifestyle Awareness: *Being in Touch With and Expressing Our Feelings*

We are aware of the importance of being in touch with and expressing our feelings. It will help if we try to allow ourselves to experience and express them without judgment or denial.

Raising Our Level of Awareness

1. Many of us learned to repress our feelings when we were very young, usually because of criticism we received for expressing them. Repressed feelings contribute to our anxiety problems.

1. It will help if we see our feelings as normal, necessary experiences and allow ourselves to express them. When this is difficult to do, we might consider keeping a journal to record them.

2. We don't always see our feelings as being valid or important, giving ourselves the message, *It's not okay to feel this way*. However, denying our feelings can leave us open to anxiety or panic.

2. It will be easier to be in touch with our feelings, and allow them to be there, if we try to see them as valid.

3. Our perfectionism keeps our feelings under control. Expressing our emotions (anger, sadness, fear) feels like losing control. We are afraid this could result in criticism, alienation, or abandonment.

3. It will help if we practice expressing our feelings even at the risk of being criticized, alienated, or abandoned.

4. As with other feelings we would rather not deal with, we tend to push feelings of guilt aside.

4. We might try to deal with guilt as we would any other emotion. Once we have faced it and worked through it, it will be easier to let go of it.

Chapter six

Strategy No. 4: Slowing Down

Strategy No. 4: *Slowing Down*

When feeling anxious, we will try to slow down, not only in our actions but in our thinking as well. When we feel a need to rush ahead, it will help if we try to focus on the moment.

At the onset of anxiety or panic, our automatic reaction is to speed up to put an end to our discomfort as soon as possible. The more we hurry, however, the more anxious we become. It's helpful to identify this need to speed up and to recognize that it's subconscious. Once we acknowledge and understand this need, we are in a position to try a different approach - slowing down.

Even when we slow down, our thoughts still tend to rush. Whether we are on the expressway or in the mall, with the first wave of anxiety or panic our mind rushes ahead to the nearest exit - signalling the need to escape - and we are caught up in a vicious circle of intense anxiety or panic. What helps is to try to slow everything down and focus on the moment, allowing each wave of anxiety to run its course. Even if we choose to leave an uncomfortable situation, it helps to escape slowly. Doing so can help us keep alert to what we are doing, as well as remind us to use the helpful Good-talk and to stay calm.

Finally, reminding ourselves to slow down will be more effective if we see it as an option and not as a must: *If I have a difficult time slowing down, so be it. But I'll try the best I can.*

Other helpful strategies include the following:

- Visualizing ourselves moving in slow motion
- Actually moving or walking in slow motion
- Visualizing ourselves moving into a panic attack rather than away from it; in effect, mentally embracing the fear

We might try to visualize ourselves slowing down in a feared situation before the actual event. This would give us some practice in dealing with the anxiety and help us cope better at the time. With some practice, and if we so choose, diaphragmatic breathing can keep us from hyperventilating. Remember, we do not have to do anything to "fix" it, but we do have the option to choose certain strategies that might be helpful.

Recovery can be a slow process and our Crap-talk tells us to seek quick solutions. As frustrating as it maybe, coming to terms with the idea that recovery takes time may be helpful. The more we slow down, the less troublesome our anxiety will be; the less hurried we are to get over our anxiety problem, the more quickly we can recover from it. If we allow ourselves to experience the process without trying to rush through it, we can actually be strengthened by it. Rushing through the recovery process is self-defeating because it denies us the opportunity to learn and grow.

Listening To Our Inner Dialogue: *Accelerating/ Slowing Down*

We tend to see speed as desirable. We believe it guarantees that we will get things done quickly and more efficiently, so the faster we get things done, the better off we will be. Our inner dialogue says, I can't let time pass, because if I do, it will pass me by. We feel that escape from an anxious situation needs to be done as quickly as possible.

Crap-talk: Accelerating	**Good-talk: SlowingDown**
1. I hate this! I wish this anxiety would go away now!	1. Wishing the anxiety away doesn't help. I'll try to slow

I've got to find a solution quickly!	down and allow it to be there.
2. I've got to get out of here! I can't take this anymore! Leaving is the fastest way to put an end to this.	2. It's okay to leave, but it helps to escape slowly.
3. I'd better hurry up before the anxiety gets worse and I have a full-blown panic attack.	3. It's better if I just take my time. Hurrying is a sure way to bring on feelings of panic.
4. If this doesn't go away soon, it will continue to get worse, and who knows what might happen to me!	4. The more I try to speed up my recovery, the more anxious I feel. It's possible that my anxiety might get worse for a while. I'll try to be okay with that.
5. Why doesn't this go away? It seems like it's going to last forever! I've got to get rid of this problem right now!	5. The less I hurry to get over this, the more quickly I'll recover.

Lifestyle Awareness: *Slowing Down*

We are aware that we have a tendency to take life at a fast pace. It will help if we try to slow down, make fewer demands on ourselves, and take time to experience the present.

Raising Our Level of Awareness

1. One of the worst problems we face is speeding up, because it constantly stirs up our anxiety.	1. We will try to be aware of our pace and practice slowing down as much as possible, even when those around us are rushing.
2. Perfectionism coerces the mind to take on more than it can handle, which only adds to the need to rush.	2. It will help if we give ourselves permission to take on less each day and then prioritize our activities.

3. We have a difficult time allowing ourselves to do nothing. We feel that every minute of our time must be productive.

4. Even when we're physically able to slow down, we often find that our thoughts are still racing.

5. We often feel like we're working within a time frame; we feel we must get on to the next task even before completing the task we're on.

6. We think that the faster we go, the more efficient we are, and that moving slowly is a sign of laziness. This king of thinking results in feelings of inadequacies.

3. We will practice taking short breaks throughout the day, allowing ourselves to do nothing.

4. We will try to slow down our thinking. If we can't, then we'll try to be okay with that.

5. We will focus on the task at hand, reminding ourselves that there's no need to rush ahead.

6. It will help if we allow ourselves to slow down, reassuring ourselves that it is not a sign of inefficiency.

It's difficult for those of us who have an anxiety disorder to think that we can benefit in any way from our anxiety problem. We're usually well into recovery, or recovered, before we're able to look back and appreciate what we've learned from our experience.

Chapter seven

Strategy No. 5: Letting Go of Control

Chapter seven

Strategy No. 5: *Letting Go of Control*

Lifestyle awareness.

With the onset of intense anxiety or panic, our first reaction is to try to stay in control. It will help if we practice letting go; the less we attempt to stay in control, the more in control we will feel.

Control is a major issue for those of us with an anxiety problem. Often feeling anxious, and therefore vulnerable, we are constantly on the guard against losing control. Loss of control can mean having a panic attack; leaving a situation because of panic, generalized anxiety, dizziness, or lightheadedness; experiencing a feeling of unreality; strangely enough, even feeling calm and relaxed. Whichever form it takes, we perceive loss of control as unacceptable. We fear that losing control will lead to a shameful conclusion that will intensify our sense of personal inadequacy.

A panic attack can seem like the ultimate in loss of control. We just aren't sure where it's going to take us or what might be waiting for us on the other side of the panic. We tell ourselves that we must do something to stop it. The most logical way, of course, would be to take control of it. However, there is nothing logical about panic attacks. The message "I must stay in control" is not very effective and usually results in the very panic attack we're trying so hard to avoid.

As illogical as it seems, the best way to "control" a panic attack is not to control it at all. In other words, the more we can let go and allow it to happen, the less likely the panic will occur. We are especially on the alert when we approach a situation in which we've panicked before. Of course, there is nothing unrealistic about expecting to panic in such situations.

Dizziness and lightheadedness can also give us the feeling of being out of control. Often we fear they will lead to fainting. Rather than taking the chance of attracting that kind of attention, we avoid going to public places where we think that might happen. We feel particularly vulnerable when the symptoms have persisted over a long period of time.

Our interpretation of what we think might be happening can be very frightening, triggering more anxiety and feelings of loss of control. What might be helpful is to give ourselves a simple explanation: *I'm feeling very anxious today. Perhaps I need to slow down.* Or, *Maybe I'm hyper-ventilating.* We then need to let go of trying to control the anxiety and give it all the room it needs; in other words, to just let it happen. We might encourage the thought *This is who I am today,* or *This is how I'm feeling right now,* and then allow ourselves to muddle through the best we can. Not trying to control the symptoms can help free us from feeling trapped.

A feeling of unreality is one of the most challenging symptoms to cope with. It is very frightening because we believe we are losing our sanity. But such feelings are not dangerous. If we can leave them alone, reassuring ourselves that they are harmless, they too will pass.

Escaping an uncomfortable situation also gives us a feeling of losing control, since we interpret it as a signal of a complete breakdown in coping skills. We tell ourselves, *If I can't stay right here and deal with this, it will get the better of me. It will continue to get worse, and I'll lose complete control over this whole situation.* Sooner or later we learn that giving ourselves permission to leave actually helps us to stay.

It makes sense that anxiety and panic can give us the feeling of being out of control, yet so can feeling calm and relaxed. Being relaxed can be uncomfortable for those of us with an anxiety problem, because we feel a need to be always on the alert for danger. We perceive tension as necessary, feeling that it is better to be tense and vigilant than to be caught off guard. It would help us if we could see that there's no need to be constantly anxious, just as there's no need to be constantly relaxed.

Listening To Our Inner Dialogue: *Controlling/Letting Go*

We believe that losing control is shameful and must be prevented, and that one way to do so is to keep tight control over our feelings and thoughts. We believe that losing control has catastrophic consequences. We believe that being in control not only averts disaster but helps keep us in a state that is beyond reproach. We're afraid that if we allow ourselves to be anxious, the anxiety will become unmanageable; we'll panic, and the panic might last forever. We tell ourselves that if we can control ourselves, we won't get anxious. However, just the opposite is true. The more we let go of control, the more in control we will feel.

Crap-talk: Controlling	Good-talk: Letting Go
1. I must not let this get out of hand! I've got to stay in control!	1. I'll try to allow myself to let go of control. The more I can let go, the better.
2. I've got to keep on top of things! I can't allow myself to give in to this problem!	2. The more I try to stay on top of this, the more of a problem it's going to be.
3. I have to be cautious or else the anxiety might suddenly catch me off guard!	3. It will help if I try to let go, since it seems like the more cautious I am, the more anxious I get.
4. I can't relax! If I relax, things might get out of hand.	4. It's okay to relax! If things should get out of hand, so be it!
5. I can't go. If I do, I might lose control and make a fool of myself.	5. The fear of making a fool of myself is only a thought. Chances are, it's not going to happen.
6. I can't leave because of these feelings. If I give in to them now, it will be just that much worse the next time!	6. I do have the option to leave, in which case I could practice being okay with leaving. Knowing that I have the option will make it easier to stay, now or any other time.

Lifestyle Awareness: *Letting Go Of Control In Our Lives*

We are always aware that we sometimes feel out of control of our lives, which can leave us feeling trapped and helpless. We will try to let go, allow for more spontaneity, and see ourselves as having options.

Raising Our Level of Awareness

1. We sometimes feel out of control in relationships in which we perceive others as being in control, e.g., in the workplace.

1. Even though we might feel out control, it will help if we try to do whatever we can to promote our sense of adequacy.

2. Our excessive need to be in control makes it difficult for us to take risks and to make changes in our lives. It promotes passivity and avoidance. Because we usually don't see ourselves as having options, we feel trapped and helpless.

2. Seeing ourselves as having options will help us reassure ourselves that we can take risks to bring about necessary changes. This will help us feel more in control of our lives.

3. We have a difficult time in situations where we really don't have control, e.g., as a passenger in a car or airplane.

3. We will try to let go and place more trust in others when we are in situations where we have no control.

4. When things do not work out the way we want them to, we tell ourselves we have to bring them under control.

4. It will help if we allow some situations to fall outside our perceived control. Where there is little we can do, it helps to let go.

Chapter eight

Strategy No. 6: *Taking Risks*

We will try to take risks rather than continually avoid places and situations where we feel anxious. It will help if we reassure ourselves that we are not in any danger and that we can function well even when we're uncomfortable.

Difficult as it may be, the best way to get through the panic is to actually go through it. We need to develop confidence in our coping skills, to know that we can make it through a panic attack, and that in spite of its intensity we can still function. Sometimes this means putting ourselves in situations where we might feel vulnerable to intense anxiety. It means taking risks.

Although risk-taking is a necessary part of our recovery, we manage to come up with any number of reasons for avoiding places where we might feel anxious or experience panic. The problem with avoidance is that our anxiety usually gets worse rather than better. Not wanting to take risks, we avoid more and more places, and our world progressively grows smaller. When we realize this is happening, we try to hold our ground so that our problem does not worsen. But this only causes more anxiety.

Unfortunately, not taking risks perpetuates this pattern of avoidance and keeps us stuck. So why do we avoid? For one thing, we're afraid that exposure to a feared situation could result in a serious setback. We think that having a bad experience might discourage us from trying again. Some of us feel that it could precipitate a physical reaction that would damage our health. Whatever the reason, we see avoidance as a form of protection.

Another reason for avoiding - one might not be aware of - is that we do not want to deal with the feeling of failure we experience when our anxiety becomes unmanageable and we feel that we have to leave the situation. In order to protect our self-esteem, we avoid taking the risk altogether.

Whatever our reason for avoiding, there is a way out of this panic-avoidance cycle. First, we need to give ourselves options, such as telling ourselves It's okay to stay and It's okay to leave. And then we need to see each risk as an opportunity to practice. When we do take risks, we expect ourselves to perform perfectly, which sets us up for failure. Seeing each risk as continued practice diminishes our perception of failure.

For example, we can practice taking the risk of going out, allowing any anxiety we might have, going though a panic attack, and staying in spite of the panic attack or accepting our decision to leave. We can also try to feel okay about ourselves when doing so. Viewing each of these options as an opportunity to practice, we can see that there is little or no possibility of failure.

At first, we might need the help of a support person, someone we feel safe with. As we gain confidence, we can begin venturing out on our own. As we gradually open ourselves to more risk-taking, we begin to realize that we can function even though we're feeling uncomfortable. It will help if we can allow ourselves to feel good about any risks we've taken regardless of the outcome (even though this is difficult for us to do).

As long as we feel that we are in some kind of danger, and as long as we insist on comfort or see the need to escape as failure, we will continue to avoid. Realizing that we do have choices in difficult situations, and seeing each situation as an opportunity to practice, can give us the confidence we need to take the risks that are necessary for recovery.

Listening To Our Inner Dialogue: *Avoidance/Exposure*

Avoidance has been a favorite strategy of ours in dealing with difficult problems. We seem to believe that avoiding problems is a way of getting rid of them and thus feeling less shame. However, avoidance strategies are harmful because they obscure problems, which then never get attended to. Especially troublesome is our avoidance of fearful thoughts. It explains, in part, why we find it difficult to make sense of our anxiety problems, and our phobias. Avoidance also diminishes our self-esteem, since we perceive ourselves as unable to cope with everyday living.

Crap-talk: Avoidance	Good-talk: Exposure
1. If I go, it will only make me feel anxious and my condition will get worse.	1. I might feel worse at first, but it's the avoidance, not the risking, that aggravates my anxiety problem.
2. I'm just not going. That way I won't have to deal with the anxiety or the feeling of failure if I should have to leave.	2. I don't have to go, but I'll probably feel bad about avoiding a difficult situation. Either way it will be good practice in dealing with my decision.
3. Maybe I'll go. I'll just tough it out. I'll put my mind on something else and try not to think about how I'm feeling!	3. Rather than trying to distract myself, I might find it more helpful to stay in touch with how I'm feeling.
4. I don't ever want to feel	4. I might not want to feel

| this way again! | anxious again, but I most likely will. It will help if I can be accepting of that. |

5. I'm leaving! I'm getting out of here before I have a full-blown panic attack!

5. It's okay to leave. I can practice being accepting of that. I don't have to stay in a difficult situation.

6. I can't leave. If I do, I'll be giving in to my fear, and it will be even more difficult to come back the next time.

6. Giving myself an out so that I don't feel trapped will make it easier to come back next time. I can even plan my escape. What matters is that I accept my decision.

Lifestyle Awareness: *Facing Difficult Situations*

We are aware that we often choose avoidance as a way of dealing with difficult situations. It would be more helpful to try to work through these difficulties. If we cannot bring about a change, it will help if we try to generate a new perception of the situation so that we will not feel trapped or helpless.

Raising Our Level of Awareness

1. We often express our feelings through silence to avoid confrontations with others. We see this as a way of keeping the peace and protecting our self-esteem from

1. We need to work through difficult situations by expressing how we feel rather than pretending the feelings don't exist or convincing ourselves that they don't

unnecessary attack.

matter.

2. We often avoid being assertive when we need to be. Assertiveness is difficult for those of us who feel we need the approval of others and do not want to rock the boat.

2. We can risk asserting ourselves in situations where we feel it might be helpful. This might mean expressing our opinion at the expense of keeping the peace.

3. We often do not see ourselves as having options, which gives us a feeling of being stuck, trapped, or helpless.

3. It would help if we could see the possibility of choices when dealing with difficult situations. If we cannot bring about a change, we might try to generate a new perception of our situation so that we will not feel trapped or helpless.

Taking it one step at a time can be an effective way of approaching a scary situation. Strategies such as slowing down and focusing on the moment can help us deal with our anxiety when taking risks.

Chapter nine

Strategy No. 7: *Allowing Catastrophic Thoughts*

When "catastrophizing" with the what-ifs, we will try to be permissive of them and not fight them. It will help to realize that they are only thoughts and that chances are they will not happen. It might also help to affirm that we carry our safety within.

Anyone who is chronically anxious or has ever had a panic attack is familiar with the what-ifs. With the slightest indication of anxiety we are quick to ask ourselves, What if this anxiety becomes unmanageable? What if I panic? What if I faint? What if I make a fool of myself? Catastrophic thoughts are not uncommon. Everyone has them at one time or another. However, they are usually taken in one's stride. Those of us with anxiety problems, on the other hand, perceive them as omens of disaster and feel we have to get rid of them. It is important for us to know that there is nothing wrong with having catastrophic thoughts and that we do not have to do anything about them. It is only when we perceive them as a problem that they become a problem.

When dealing with catastrophic thoughts, two strategies might help: (1) perceiving the catastrophic thought as normal and acceptable, and (2) making use of the catastrophic thought as an opportunity to figure out what we might do to get through a feared situation before we're actually faced with it. For instance:

Q.   What if I faint?

A.   I've never fainted before and chances are it's not going to happen how. If it does, someone will help me. I hate the thought of fainting, but that's all it is - a thought.

Q.   What if I get anxious while I'm driving and get into an accident?

A.   This is only a thought about causing an accident. If I get anxious, I will try to go with the feelings. I can always pull over if the anxiety becomes unmanageable.

Dealing with persistent and unexplainable symptoms, and at times a sense of impending doom, is it any wonder that we become concerned about them and ask what if? We will most likely experience a lot of panic attacks before we are reassured that the what-ifs are unlikely to happen.

It can help if we allow the catastrophic thoughts to be there, while at the same time encouraging an inner dialogue that is in direct competition with them. Being permissive of catastrophic thoughts will diminish their troublesome nature.

We might gently affirm that we carry our safety within, that our safety is not back home or in any other given place, and that what we are experiencing is only a feeling. This will not be easy at first, but the thought itself might help keep us from frightening ourselves further.

What-ifs are not always questions about what to do. For instance, when we ask, *What if I panic?* we're not necessarily asking what we should do in case of a panic attack. What we're actually saying is *I must not panic* or *I've got to control the panic.* At this point it doesn't really help to become rational. What helps is to try seeing the thought of panicking as acceptable.

Catastrophic thoughts will probably continue, but hopefully to a less troublesome degree. It will help if we are patient with the what-ifs, allowing them to be there and realizing that they are normal. Catastrophic thoughts are not about real events, they are thoughts that encourage us to prepare ourselves to cope with anticipated events before they actually occur.

Listening to Our Inner Dialogue: *Distracting/Inviting*

Fearful thoughts and catastrophic thoughts are honest-to-goodness emotions. We don't need to alter, change, control, or get rid of them - nor could we if we wanted to. Rather than presenting a problem, they can actually serve a purpose. If we listen to what they tell us, we can become better prepared for anticipated events that are scaring us. For example, we can engage in some anticipatory problem-solving, which will help us cope better.

Crap-talk: Distracting	Good-talk: Inviting
1. I'll try to put my mind on something else! I'm just not going to allow these thoughts anymore!	1. Trying to distract myself doesn't always work very well. Besides, they're only thoughts. It helps if I allow them to be there.
2. I've got to stop worrying so much!	2. I'll start worrying less when I stop trying so hard to control my thoughts. It might help if I see worry as an option, and see that it sometimes serves a purpose.
3. I have to stop thinking this way!	3. Telling myself that I have to stop these thoughts only

makes matters worse.

4. I shouldn't have these thoughts. There must be something terribly wrong with me for thinking this way.

4. They're only thoughts. It's okay to have them! It doesn't mean that there's something terribly wrong with me.

5. What if my worst fear really does happen? I'd better make sure it doesn't!

5. So be it! I'll deal with it the best I can when the time comes.

Lifestyle Awareness: *Allowing Unwanted Thoughts*

We are aware that our tendency to catastrophize makes it difficult to be receptive to positive outcomes. It will help if we are permissive of our thoughts, both positive and negative, rather than feeling that we have to block them out or replace them with other thought.

Raising Our Level of Awareness

1. Worrying can sometimes give us a feeling of having control over an otherwise out-of-control situation. Sometimes we feel that by worrying we can actually keep bad things from happening.

1. It will help if we realize that we cannot control future events by worrying about them. However, we will try to allow worry as an option, since not allowing worry - fearful that it might get out of hand - is the same as not allowing thoughts.

2. We sometimes worry to a point where it no longer

2. It will help if we realize that there is a point where

seems helpful. We just don't know when to let go of it.

we can let go of worry: when we have worried over a long period of time, when the worry is about something that is completely out of our control, or when it's about an event in the distant future.

3Positive thinking can be challenging for those of us who are phobic and/or depressed. When we have difficulty conjuring up positive thoughts to replace the negative ones, we feel that we have failed and that there must be something terribly wrong with us.

3. Realizing that it is difficult to simply replace a negative thought, we might think in terms of being more receptive to positive thoughts, seeing them as options and not as "have-tos". It will help if we can feel okay about ourselves when positive thoughts are difficult to come by.

4. We tend to resist unwanted thoughts by trying to block them out or by frantically trying to replace them with other thoughts.

4. It will help if we allow all thoughts, even those that seem troublesome, rather than blocking them out or doing battle with them. We will try to see them for what they are - just thoughts.

Chapter ten

Strategy No. 8:*Learning and Talking About Our Anxiety Disorder*

We will try to develop a more helpful attitude toward our anxiety disorder by learning more about it, thus removing the veil of mystery. By talking about it, we also lift the burden of a deep, dark secret.

The fear we experience during an anxiety or panic episode is especially alarming because we do not know what is happening to us. Unfortunately, most of the explanations we come up with on our own frighten us even more, and we do one of two things: either we avoid learning anything about our problem, or we seek excessively complex explanations, which causes us to become more frustrated. In both cases, we're unable to come up with simple and accurate answers.

The more inquisitive we are about our anxiety or panic attacks, and the more we learn about our disorder, the less alarmed we will be by its apparent mysteries. Just knowing that our problem has a name helps, but all too often our knowledge stops there. It's not uncommon to hear such statements as "Perhaps the less I hear about this the better," or, "I'm afraid that if I read about this problem, I'll pick up new symptoms and continue to get worse." This is just one more way of avoiding. It's like saying, "If I don't think about my anxiety, it will go away." Unfortunately, it doesn't work that way.

Taking away the mystery will help alleviate the fear. We might begin by seeing an anxiety or panic attack as an interesting phenomenon that comes from within, one that we ourselves have set into motion with our thoughts, rather than seeing it as a frightening attack that comes from out of the blue. Leaving us bewildered and out of control.

Learning about our anxiety and panic removes much of the mystery. Many books and articles provide insight and suggestions for dealing with anxiety disorders. It will help if we approach our quest for knowledge gradually, without the attitude of "I have to get over this problem once and for all." What is important is to open ourselves to information about our problem and to be willing to risk learning more about it.

Discussing our anxiety disorder with others is difficult, since we're not really sure ourselves what's happening. Unfortunately, whenever we carry a deep, dark secret we take on the extra burden of shame which only adds to our anxiety. Our inner dialogue is permeated with such thoughts as

I shouldn't feel this way, *Something is terribly wrong with me*, and *What will people think?* If we haven't come to terms with the fact that we have an anxiety disorder, how can we possibly discuss it with others who have little idea of what we're talking about and who, we feel, might stand in judgment of us?

At the same time, it isn't necessary to rush into the boss's office the first day on the job and announce that we are prone to intense anxiety or panic attacks that seem to come out of nowhere at the most inappropriate times. We might begin by confiding in a spouse or close friend. Being somewhat casual or matter-of-fact about our situation can help put the listener at ease. For instance, when having lunch with a friend, we might say, "I sometimes feel panicky in restaurants. So if I step out for a minute, you don't have to worry." If our attitude says that it's no big deal, chances are that the other person will see it that way too. Being able to talk about our anxiety disorder as just another fact of life tends to make it just that.

Trying to see our situation in humorous terms can also help put things into better perspective. It is possible to find humor in having driven thirty miles out of the way to avoid an expressway or having climbed seven flights of stairs to avoid taking an elevator. If we could not laugh at our plight, its reality would be overwhelming.

Listening To Our Inner Dialogue: *Avoidance/Exposure*

Avoiding an understanding of how our problem works can be very appealing, but usually the problem only becomes mysterious and alarming. On the other hand, trying to understand and analyze the problem too deeply can be an exercise in continuous frustration. Perhaps our goal can be to arrive at a simple and accurate understanding of what is troubling us.

Crap-talk: Avoidance	Good-talk: Exposure
1. It would be better not to read anything about this problem, or it might get worse.	1. My problem might get worse for a while, but that's only because I'm facing it and trying to deal with it.
2. I don't want to hear anyone else talk about this, because I just might pick up their symptoms.	2. While it's possible for me to pick up symptoms, it's better to take that risk than to keep running away from the problem.
3. If I just don't think about it, the problem will eventually go away.	3. Trying not to think about my problem doesn't seem to help. As a matter of fact, the more I try not to think about it, the worse it gets.

4. If people find about this, they're going to think there's something wrong with me.

4. My real concern is how I might feel about people having that thought about me. I'll try to feel okay about myself regardless of what others think about me.

5. It's best that I don't talk about this to anyone, because of what people might think.

5. It might help to open up to a close friend, someone I can trust. The more I try to hide this, the more anxious I seem to feel.

Lifestyle Awareness: *Understanding Events in Our Lives*

We are aware that we sometimes avoid processing difficult events in our lives by not thinking about them or by distorting their meaning. It will help if we take a good look at them and try to see the meaning that they have for us.

Raising Our Level of Awareness

1. We often avoid processing difficult events in our lives by not thinking about them. For example, if we are having a conflict with someone at work, we avoid trying to understand what the conflict is about and therefore avoid finding ways to resolve it.

1. It would help if we took a good look at difficult events in our lives, understood what they were about, and tried to resolve them.

2. If something bothers us,

2. Rather than explaining a

we often distort its meaning or try not to think about it so that it no longer bothers us.

problem to ourselves in a way that completely distorts its meaning, it is much more helpful to explain it in a way that makes simple sense of it and then accept it for what it is.

3. We often experience considerable stress when a problem arises, but we resort to relieving the symptoms of stress rather than face the events that are creating it.

3. It would be helpful to allow ourselves to feel the physical manifestations of stress while trying to attend to its cause.

Chapter eleven

Strategy No. 9: *Keeping Our Expectations Low*

When approaching a situation where we feel anxious, we will try to take it one step at a time, keeping our expectations low. It will help if we think of it as an opportunity to practice.

Just as we tend to expect ourselves to do well in general, we also expect to do well when we are in situations where we feel anxious. By setting our expectations high (and not allowing for any discomfort), we believe that we will raise our level of performance. However, just the opposite is true. When we raise our expectations, we only add more anxiety to an already distressed system. On the other hand, the less we expect to do well, the less pressure we put on ourselves and the more efficiently we'll be able to perform. In other words, the more we can allow ourselves not to do well, the better we'll do.

We tend to set high expectations in situations such as returning to a place where we had done particularly well. We feel that because we handled our anxiety well the last time, we should be able to do well again, if not better. The same holds true for travelling. If the outbound trip went well, we expect the return trip to go well too. With our expectations up, however, the least sign of discomfort can trigger intense anxiety. What happens the second time around is that we automatically raise our expectations of doing well. It will help if we see each experience as practice and continue to lower our expectations by allowing ourselves to be uncomfortable. We forget that the reason we coped well before was that we lowered our expectations. Having forgotten that, the Crap-talk returns and we are convinced that the repeat should be a piece of cake.

The pressure generated by high expectations causes us to respond to the slightest discomfort with great alarm. During these times we are most vulnerable to panic attacks, exactly when we least expect them. It is when we expect the panic attacks to happen, and allow the anticipation that we cope the best, that panic attacks are the least likely to occur.

As perfectionists, we expect not only a high score in handling our anxiety but a complete recovery - as soon as possible. Unfortunately, the more effort we put forth, the more frustrated we become. Here again, we need to lower our expectations and allow as much time as necessary for recovery. If we can reassure ourselves that we will be able to manage and that our difficulties with anxiety will improve with time, we may feel less trapped in a situation that once seemed unmanageable.

So as we approach each situation where we feel anxious, it will help if we try to take it one step at a time, keeping our expectations low and allowing for any discomfort. Seeing the situation as an opportunity to practice will help us in our recovery.

Listening To Our Inner Dialogue: *Raising/Lowering Expectations*

We tend to think that the way to deal with any problem is to raise expectations as much as possible: the higher our expectations, the better we'll be able to solve a problem. We believe that if we set 100 percent success as a minimum expectation, we'll be more likely to cope with maximum efficiency. Failure must be prevented at all costs, because failure is shameful and therefore unacceptable. Moreover, we believe the more we fail, the more unmanageable our problem will become. Thus we believe we should do our best to avoid failure. It might seem paradoxical, but the more we lower our expectations and allow for failure, the less anxiety we'll experience and the better we'll do.

Crap-talk:Raising Expectations	Good-talk:Lowering Expectations
1. I must not get anxious. I must not fail again!	1. Chances are, I will be anxious. However, the more I can allow the anxiety, the better. It will help if I can see this as a chance to practice having these feelings, rather than as a failure.
2. I did well the last time I was here, so this should be easy.	2. Sometimes it's more difficult the next time out, because I automatically raise my expectations. It will help if I can continue to keep my expectations low.
3. I should try harder!	3. Sometimes it's best to let up a little and not try so hard, since the harder I try, the worse it seems to get.
4. I must not escape to avoid this anxiety or it will be that much more difficult to come back the next time.	4. It's important to take risks, but telling myself that I have to stay only makes me feel trapped. If I give myself the option to leave, it might make it easier for me to come back the next time.
5. If I can't do it well, I shouldn't even try.	5. It doesn't have to be great —or even good. Just taking the risk is helpful.
6. If I'm not succeeding, it's because I'm not trying hard enough!	6. If I'm not succeeding, it might be because I'm trying too hard. Sometimes it's best to do nothing and just muddle through.

Lifestyle Awareness: *Allowing Imperfection*

We are aware of our need for perfectionism. It will help if we allow ourselves to be average rather than to continually strive for perfection. We might remind ourselves that making mistakes does not have to affect our self-worth.

Raising Our Level of Awareness

1. Our perfectionism may be a sign of low self-esteem. As children we may have been denied the freedom to fail.

1. We can try to lower our expectations and allow for failure. It will help if we see failure as an opportunity for growth.

2. Our perfectionism can sometimes be a result of trying to make up for what we perceive to be defective in us. We feel that making a mistake contributes to a further loss of self-esteem.

2. It helps if we realize that our desire to be perfect can be self-defeating. In other words, the harder we try, the more inefficient we'll become.

3. We impose high standards on ourselves; if we don not live up to them, we feel our self-worth will diminish.

3. We can try to develop more reasonable or manageable expectations. We might even challenge ourselves to be average rather than continually striving for perfection.

4. We are fearful that we might panic in a crisis.

4. It might help to remind ourselves that we usually function well in a crisis situation, since our expectations at that time are lowered.

When going into a feared situation, we often test ourselves to see how well we can do. With our expectations high however, we react to the slightest sign of discomfort.

Chapter twelve

Strategy No. 10: *Accepting Setbacks*

We will try to accept setbacks as a normal and necessary part of our recovery, trying to see them as temporary. It might help to remind ourselves that even though we feel as if we're starting over, we never really go back to square one.

The recovery process is never easy. We seem to do well for a while, and then suddenly the rug is pulled out from under us. What might have been easy yesterday is difficult today. Just when we thought that we were finally getting better, those all-too-familiar feelings of intense anxiety or panic seem to come out of nowhere. Our self-talk reverts to *Oh, no, not again! I'm never going to get over this! I'm right back where I started!* Along with having feelings of failure and discouragement, we're consumed with the fear that we are in a continuous cycle of being out of control and there is nothing we can do about it.

The fear of being out of control is a particularly disturbing part of setbacks. Not only do we feel extremely vulnerable, but the what-ifs abound: *What if this sets in for good? What if it continues to get worse?* And so on. We try hard to eliminate the catastrophic thoughts. Our inclination is to hang on tight, stay in control, and hold our ground to avoid backtracking. What might be helpful at this point, however, is to do just the opposite: give ourselves permission not to be in control, and even to lose some ground if necessary. It will help if we remind ourselves that in spite of a feeling of losing ground, we will not go back to square one and we are still making progress.

The truth is, we never really go back to where we started; it only seems that way because we've had a short reprieve and felt like a "regular" person again. And now the situation seems worse by comparison. Besides, how can we possibly go back to square one when we've learned so much about our problem and how to deal with it? Our perception is beginning to change, and it can never be quite the same as it was when we first started experiencing panic attacks.

It helps to know that there are reasons for setbacks. Usually they signal the need to slow down. On days when we're feeling good and we're able to get out to do some of the things we haven't been able to do for a while, we tend to overdo it, which leaves us feeling depleted. Also, when all has gone well for a while, our expectations go up and we might tell ourselves, Well I did this last week and had no problem. This should be a piece of cake. When we have such high expectations and do not allow for any discomfort, the least sign of a symptom can throw us into a whirlwind of anxiety or panic. Whether we leave or stay matters little. We feel as though we've failed once again, and the feeling of being out of control becomes demoralizing.

How we perceive or interpret our setbacks can make a difference to how troublesome they are or how long they last. Seeing them as isolated events rather than continuous chain reactions can help take away some of the fear that they are setting in for good. Our self-talk might be, *This is today. It has no bearing on what will happen tomorrow*, or *This too shall pass.* We might wish to remind ourselves that setbacks are a normal and necessary part of our recovery. We might even see them as opportunities for continued practice in working through the anxiety or panic attacks. The more we practice being permissive of the panic feelings, the less frightening they become and the more confidence we gain in working with them. We have learned to frighten ourselves. It will take time to relearn a new kind of inner dialogue, one that is reassuring and supportive. As we approach each new plateau, we can remind ourselves that the setback is a transition period that allows us to make continued progress.

Listening To Our Inner Dialogue: *Non-acceptance/Acceptance*

Setbacks are normal. They are opportunities to practice dealing with difficult situations. Since it's impossible to get well without setbacks, it's important that we have them. But when we do have them, it feels as if we're back to square one. In reality, setbacks are preludes to progressive phases. When we have setbacks, it helps if we let them be, not trying so hard to get rid of them or control them, but letting them take their natural course. Before we know it, they subside, and we are on our way to making more progress.

Crap-talk: Non-acceptance	Good-talk: Acceptance
1. I'm never going to get over this. I'm right back where I started!	1. This gets better, but it takes time. It helps if I can try to accept that. Although it may seem like I'm back to where I started, I am making progress.
2. I can't afford to have this problem anymore. It has to stop right now!	2. Telling myself that it has to stop only makes matters worse. It's better to try to allow the anxiety to take its course.
3. Enough of this! I just can't take this anymore!	3. It's going to happen whether I want it to or not. It

	helps if I try to accept that.
4. I'm always going to be this way!	4. I'll try to be open to the thought that it might be this way for a long time. But it will improve.
5. I've just got to be normal!	5. What is normal? Everyone has some kind of problem. Mine is having a difficult time dealing with unmanageable fear or panic attacks.
6. Why can't this problem just go away and never come back?	6. This isn't just coming from out of the blue. There's a reason why I'm having these feelings. It might help if I slow down or perhaps take a look at what's happening in my life that keeps me anxious.

Lifestyle Awareness: *Giving Ourselves the Freedom to Fail*

We are aware that we have a difficult time dealing with failure, seeing it as further evidence of low self-worth. It will help if we give ourselves the freedom to fail, considering it an opportunity for growth.

Raising Our Level of Awareness

1. Our high standards of perfectionism do not readily allow for failure. We tend to see it as further proof of our inadequacies or defectiveness. We have to succeed at work, we have to be perfect parents, we must even excel at our hobbies.

1. It will help to generate the thought, I don't have to succeed, and if I fail, that would provide me with a valuable learning experience.

2. We tend to associate our self-worth with how well we perform. Rather than feeling bad about ourselves, we choose not to perform at all.

2. We might try to remind ourselves that anyone can feel good when he or she does well. The real challenge is to feel all right about ourselves when we don't do well.

3. Our fear of failure can keep us from taking risks and doing the things that we really want to do in life.

3. We will try to take more risks, allowing ourselves the freedom to fail, seeing it as an opportunity for growth. We might even imagine the worst that could happen and then allow for that possibility.

Setbacks can be alarming, but it will help if we try to accept them.

Chapter thirteen

Strategy No. 11: *Taking the Time Limit out of Recovery*

We will try to take the time limit out of our recovery, seeing it as open-ended. It will help if we try to accept where we are right now without comparing ourselves with past progress, and at the same time, try to be accepting of the possibility of any future anxiety.

Among the many fears we have as anxiety or panic sufferers, one is that our condition will set in for good and grow increasingly worse until we are completely out of control. We find ourselves making comparisons, reminding ourselves of all the things we used to be able to do and can't do now. We then continue to frighten ourselves with the thought of how much worse it might be in the future. It will help if we allow that thought to be there, and then remind ourselves to try to be more accepting of our situation as it was, as it is now, and as it might be.

Wanting a quick recovery, we tend to place a time limit on our progress. We tell ourselves, *I'd better be over this in six months*, and then we think, *But what if I'm not?* Unfortunately, a time limit slows down the recovery process by imposing restrictions on us and burdening us with more pressures. It can also give us a feeling of being trapped, which only adds to our anxiety.

Keeping it open-ended (not putting it into a time frame) can do much to alleviate this feeling of being trapped. It gives us more options. We can begin by slowing down. We no longer have to hurry to get better, since there's plenty of time and it's no longer an all-or-nothing situation. With an attitude of acceptance, we might tell ourselves, *This is who I am today. So be it.* We might try to see this as a time to reflect on what is happening in our lives that is causing so much distress; for instance, personal issues that we might be dealing with, or perhaps not dealing with. It would help if we could take each day as it comes, accepting where we are right now in our recovery, without unduly analyzing, comparing, or judging. Going to bed at night unwilling to face the anxiety that might be there the next morning is a sure way to make it happen. The key is accepting that it probably will be there tomorrow, and for any number of mornings after that.

The possibility that our recovery will be a long process is very discouraging. However, we have learned that our anxiety and panic attacks are manageable and that we can still function in spite of them. When we lower our expectations and let time take care of itself, our difficulties with anxiety will get better, and we can be reassured that as life goes on, we will still be a part of it.

Listening To Our Inner Dialogue: *Perfectionism/Non-perfectionism*

When we're phobic, we perceive time in an extremely strict manner. We see it as something we need to control. We want to make certain that future events happen exactly the way we want them to. All this adds to our state of persistent self-aggravation. We would do much better if we allowed time and future events to take their natural course.

Crap-talk: Perfectionism	Good-talk:Non-perfectionism
1. I'm always going to have this problem. It's never going to get any better!	1. It's only natural that I have this thought. It helps if I can see it as that - a thought! With time and patience, it does get better.
2. I'm afraid this will continue to get worse until I'm completely out of control!	2. It's true that it might get worse. In fact, at times it probably will. It helps if I can allow that to happen and remind myself that relapsing is a normal part of the recovery process.
3. If it's this bad now, how	3. How I'm feeling right now

much worse will it be in six months?

has no bearing on how I might feel six months from now. For all I know, I'll feel better tomorrow.

4. I used to be able to drive across the state. Now I can't even make it as far as the corner store.

4. With practice, I will be able to get to the store again, and I will be able to travel long distances as well.

5. I'd better be over this in six months. But what if I'm not?

5. It helps to think of my recovery as open-ended. Regardless of how long it takes, I will get better.

6. I can make it to the grocery store now, but I still can't drive on the expressway.

6. I'll give myself credit for being able to get to the grocery store, and try to be okay about not driving on the expressway. I'll drive on the expressway when I'm ready.

Lifestyle Awareness: *Living One Day At a Time*

We are aware that it helps to live one day at a time, while slowly coming to terms with the past and letting the future take care of itself.

Raising Our Level of Awareness

1. Even though we know that we can't change the past, we tend not to accept troubling past events.

1. It will help if we try to work through past events that are troubling. When we accept them, we will be able to let go of them.

2. We can feel trapped by our

2. Rather than repressing

past because we are unwilling to process the meanings it has for us. For example, we are often unwilling to make a connection between the trauma or abuse of our childhood and our problem with anxiety.

these past experiences, we fight find it helpful to try to see their relationship to the present.

3. We separate ourselves from the mainstream of life. We have a tendency to watch life go by, rather than actually becoming part of it.

3. We will try to spontaneously get into the course of our life without waiting for things to improve.

One of the most difficult things for us to do is to take recovery out of a time frame. It's so tempting to set goals for ourselves and think that we should be well within a given period of time.

Chapter fourteen

Strategy No. 12:

No Longer Anticipating Panic Attacks

Chapter fourteen
Strategy No. 12:*No Longer Anticipating Panic Attacks*

During our process of recovery, we can reach a point where we no longer anticipate the occurrence of panic attacks. When we no longer care whether we panic, the attacks will eventually subside.

It is hard to believe that we could ever have a positive attitude toward something that affects our lives so dramatically as recurring panic attacks. However, with continued acceptance, repeated practice, and a supportive inner dialogue that allows us to experience the attacks, they tend to lose their uniqueness and eventually their power.

How can this be possible, we might ask, when we're unable to do something as simple as drive a car or shop for groceries without feeling as if we're going to faint, go crazy, or die? And how can telling ourselves that it's okay to be anxious possibly make a difference when we don't really feel that way? The fact is that even though permissive thoughts do not always bring about immediate success, with repeated practice they eventually help lower our level of concern. Very gradually, the more permissive we are of anxious feelings, the less attention we pay to them, not by denying them or distracting ourselves from them, but by allowing them to come to us and even trouble us.

Believability comes with repeated reassurance that our anxiety does not represent danger, and that we will be okay. We can remind ourselves that we've had many panic attacks before and have always survived. This will not be easy, because no matter how many panic attacks we've experienced in the past, the big what-if is always there to frighten us: Well, the last one was just a panic attack, but what if this time it's the real thing? We can't help wondering if our lives will continually be overshadowed by a fear of the next panic episode. Somewhere during the process of our recovery, however, we may reach a point where we are more receptive to the occurrence of panic attacks and therefore no longer devastated by them. It is then that they cease to be so troublesome to us and we find ourselves no longer concerned about whether or not we panic.

Before this happens, however, we've usually weathered any number of panic attacks with a 100 percent record of survival. We've gained an understanding of our body's reaction to stress and the physical symptoms of a panic episode. All of this has helped bring down our level of concern. With repeated practice of accepting and allowing the feelings, we emerge with confidence not only that we can survive the panic attacks, but that they are actually manageable. When we've reached the point where we're able to let go of the fear and no longer live in anticipation of the next

panic attack, we know that we are well on our way to recovery.

It's as though we've gained a new perception of what is
happening to us. The panic attacks are no longer a threat to
our well-being, nor are they a focus of our lives. We no
longer go through the day waiting for the next attack to occur; instead, we adopt the attitude that if it happens, it happens. We're able to get on with our life and take more risks
with a minimum of avoidance. The more we let go of the
fear, the less frequently the panic attacks occur, until they
eventually subside.

Listening To Our Inner Dialogue: *Non-
permissive/Permissive*

The more permissive we are about panic attacks, the less
troublesome they are. In the beginning, it is common to
perceive our panic attacks as having catastrophic signific-
ance, even though they are essentially harmless. What
causes problems for us is that we are troubled by them. We
need to keep practicing the thought, *It's all right to have
panic attacks*. That takes the power out of them, and they
gradually cease to bother us. When we are no longer

troubled by them, it no longer matters to us whether or not we panic.

Crap-talk:Non-permissive	Good-talk: Permissive
1. This is probably only a panic attack, but then again, what if this time I'm really going to faint (or die or go crazy)?	1. I've had this feeling many times before. So what else is new? I'll try not to fight it and just let it happen.
2. This is terrible! This is never going to go away! It's always going to be like this.	2. It's very possible that this will continue for some time. It will help if I can be accepting of that. But eventually it will change.
3. What if I keep having these panicky feelings?	3. The more I can allow them to happen, the better.
4. I hate this! I just can't keep letting this happen!	4. Fighting it is only going to make it worse. The best thing I can do is to just let it happen. If I panic, I panic!
5. Whatever is wrong with me must be very complex. They'll never be able to figure it our, and I'll have this forever.	5. What is wrong with me is complex, but not mysterious or hopeless. With time and patience, it will get better.

Lifestyle Awareness: *Allowing More Flexibility In Our Lives*

We are aware that we have difficulty being flexible and that we tend to see things in all-or-nothing terms. It will help if we try to be less absolute in our thinking, allowing more flexibility in our lives.

Raising Our Level of Awareness

1. We do not easily allow flexibility, which often leads us to feeling stuck.

1. When confronted with problems, we will try to see that we have options and that we are free to make choices. Our unwillingness to do so leads us to feeling stuck.

2. We often think in terms of black and white without allowing for any gray areas; we see things as either right or wrong, or good or bad.

2. It will help if we become more aware of our rigid thinking and try to see the possibility of more gray areas in our lives.

3. We tend to impose rigid rules and standards on ourselves, allowing no deviations.

3. We will try to flow with life rather than be constantly constrained by rigid and/or self-imposed rules.

4. We have a hard time being open to a less-than-perfect solution to a problem and therefore tend to give up.

4. Realizing that this is a result of our all-or-nothing thinking, we will try not to insist on always finding the perfect solution to a problem.

Chapter Fifteen

Final Strategy
Reaching out to Others

Chapter fifteen

Final Strategy: *Reaching Out To Others*

As we gain a better understanding of our anxiety problem and move ahead in our recovery, we can continue to benefit by reaching out to others who need support and encouragement.

We have learned that we are not alone, that our problem has a name, that others experience many of the same symptoms and are concerned about the problem of avoidance. We are aware of the importance of accepting, allowing, and taking risks. As we continue to practice a nurturing inner dialogue and helpful strategies in dealing with anxiety and panic attacks, our perception of what is happening to us is gradually changing. The more we learn about our anxiety problem, the less of a mystery it becomes. Perhaps we are even beginning to talk about our fear, after having kept it a secret for so long.

Those who have made progress in their own recovery often want to help those who are still struggling. Perhaps it is because they can relate to the feeling of isolation, the overwhelming fear of loss of control, and the sense of grief over the lost person they once knew. For whatever reason, when they reach out to help others, they also help themselves.

They can help other anxiety and panic sufferers by sharing the strategies and inner dialogue that have helped them through difficult situations, and by giving others encouragement and support. In a group situation, they are able to see the progress they have made when new members share their experiences, and they will benefit from seeing that what has worked for them can work for others as well. Just simply being there reassures them that they are not alone.

Here are four effective ways of reaching out to others:

- Share positive experiences such as risk-taking, effective inner dialogue, and other helpful strategies. (To prevent adding to the other person's distress, avoid symptom-swapping and becoming preoccupied with the problem.)

- Share information about helpful books and articles on anxiety and phobias.

- Offer to go out together into public places to practice newly learned strategies.

- Organize a support group.

People suffering from anxiety and panic attacks are looking for answers, but more than that, they are reaching out for a sense of hope. Those people who have made it through the rough times can give others that hope by sharing their experiences and knowledge. Through your example, many will find comfort in knowing that recovery is possible.

Bibliography

Bibliography

Bemis, Judith and Barrada, Amr. *Embracing the Fear: Learning to Manage Anxiety and Panic Attacks.*
Minnesota: Hazelden, 1994.

Kushner, M.G., Sher, K.J., and Beitman, B.D. *"The Relation Between Alcohol Problems and Anxiety Disorders."*
The American Journal of Psychiatry *147* (1990): 685-695.

Shipko, Stuart. *Surviving Panic Disorder: What You Need To Know.*
Bloomington, IN:
1st Books Library, 2003.

Swede, Shirley and Jaffe, Seymour. *The Panic Attack Recovery Book.*
New York:
New American Library, 2000.

Trickett, Shirley. *Panic Attacks: A Natural Approach, Second Edition.*
Berkeley, CA:
Ulysses Press, 1999.

Weinstock, Lorna and Gilman, Eleanor. *Overcoming Panic Disorder: A Woman's Guide.*
Chicago:
Contemporary Books, 1998.

Wilson, R. Reid. *Don't Panic: Taking Control of Anxiety Attacks.*
New York:
Harper Collins, 1996.